Winsome Pinnock

THE AUTHENTICATOR

NICK HERN BOOKS

London

www.nickhernbooks.co.uk

A Nick Hern Book

The Authenticator first published in Great Britain in 2026 as a paperback original by Nick Hern Books Limited, The Glasshouse, 49a Goldhawk Road, London W12 8QP

The Authenticator copyright © 2026 Winsome Pinnock

Winsome Pinnock has asserted her moral right to be identified as the author of this work

Cover photography (Rakie Ayola, Sylvestra Le Touzel and Cherrelle Skeete) by Blacksocks; art direction and graphic design by National Theatre Graphic Design Studio

Designed and typeset by Nick Hern Books, London
Printed in the UK by Mimeo Ltd, Huntingdon, Cambridgeshire PE29 6XX

A CIP catalogue record for this book is available from the British Library

ISBN 978 1 83904 523 3

CAUTION All rights whatsoever in this play are strictly reserved. Requests to reproduce the text in whole or in part should be addressed to the publisher. This book may not be used, in whole or in part, for the development or training of artificial intelligence technologies or systems.

Amateur Performing Rights Applications for performance, including readings and excerpts, by amateurs in the English language throughout the world should be addressed to the Performing Rights Department, Nick Hern Books, The Glasshouse, 49a Goldhawk Road, London W12 8QP, *tel* +44 (0)20 8749 4953, *email* rights@nickhernbooks.co.uk, except as follows:

Australia: ORiGiN Theatrical, Level 1, 213 Clarence Street, Sydney NSW 2000, *tel* +61 (2) 8514 5201, *email* enquiries@originmusic.com.au, *web* www.origintheatrical.com.au

New Zealand: Play Bureau, 20 Rua Street, Mangapapa, Gisborne, 4010, *tel* +64 21 258 3998, *email* info@playbureau.com

United States and Canada: Casarotto Ramsay and Associates Ltd, see details below

Professional Performing Rights Applications for performance by professionals in any medium and in any language throughout the world (including by stock companies in the USA and Canada) should be addressed to Casarotto Ramsay and Associates Ltd, *email* rights@casarotto.co.uk, www.casarotto.co.uk

No performance of any kind may be given unless a licence has been obtained. Applications should be made before rehearsals begin. Publication of this play does not necessarily indicate its availability for amateur performance.

www.nickhernbooks.co.uk/environmental-policy

Nick Hern Books' authorised representative in the EU is
Easy Access System Europe – Mustamäe tee 50, 10621 Tallinn, Estonia
email gpsr.requests@easproject.com

WINSOME PINNOCK

Winsome Pinnock's stage plays include an adaptation of Malorie Blackman's *Pig Heart Boy* (Unicorn Theatre/Sheffield Theatres and Children's Theatre Partnership), which won the 2025 UK Theatre Award for Best Show for Children & Young People; *Rockets and Blue Lights* (National Theatre, Manchester Royal Exchange and BBC Radio 3); *One Under* (Tricycle Theatre, and Graeae UK tour); *Leave Taking* (Liverpool Playhouse Theatre, National Theatre, Belgrade Theatre Coventry, Lyric Theatre Hammersmith and the Bush Theatre); *Una Calling* (Shakespeare's Globe); *Glutathione* (Young Vic); *The Principles of Cartography* (Bush Theatre); *Tituba* (Hampstead Theatre); *Cleaning Up* and *Taken* (for Clean Break at Ovalhouse Theatre); *IDP* (Tricycle Theatre); *The Stowaway* (play for young people, Plymouth Theatre); *Beg Borrow or Steal* (Kuumba Community Arts Centre); *Water* (Tricycle Theatre); *Talking in Tongues* (Royal Court Theatre Upstairs); *Mules* (Royal Court Theatre Upstairs and Clean Break Theatre); *Can You Keep a Secret?* (Connections at National Theatre); *A Rock in Water* and *A Hero's Welcome* (Royal Court Theatre); *The Wind of Change* (Half Moon Theatre) and *Picture Palace* (Women's Theatre Group).

Radio plays include *Faith, Hope and Glory*, which received the Outstanding Contribution award in the 2026 BBC Audio Drama Awards; *Leave Taking*; *Madame Tempey*; *Singin' and Swingin' and Gettin' Merry Like Christmas* (adapted from Maya Angelou's autobiography); *Clean Trade*; *Her Father's Daughter*; *Let Them Call it Jazz* (adapted from a short story by Jean Rhys); *Indiana* (adapted from the novel by George Sand); *The Dinner Party, Something Borrowed, Water* (Radio 4) and *Lazarus* (Radio 3).

Rockets and Blue Lights received the 2018 Alfred Fagon Award. A Manchester Royal Exchange Theatre performance of the play was transposed to radio as part of the Lockdown Theatre Festival produced by BBC Radio 3 and 4. The audio version of the play won an Offie in 2021. Pinnock's other awards include the George Devine Award, Pearson Plays on Stage Award for best play of the year, and the Unity Theatre Trust Award. She received a special commendation from the Susan Smith Blackburn Prize. She was Senior Visiting Fellow at Cambridge University and writer-in-residence at Holloway Prison, Clean Break Theatre Company, Royal Court Theatre, Kuumba Arts Community Centre, Tricycle Theatre and the National Theatre Studio. She was UNESCO Fellow at University of East Anglia and in 2020 became a Fellow of the Royal Society of Literature. Her play *Leave Taking* received a major revival at the Bush Theatre in 2018 and a revival of *One Under* toured nationally and at the Arcola Theatre, London, by Graeae Theatre Company in autumn 2019. In 2021 she was an inaugural recipient of Jeremy O. Harris and New York Theatre Workshop's Golden and Ruth Harris Commission. In 2022 she was the recipient of the Windham Campbell Prize.

Other Titles in this Series

Waleed Akhtar
THE ART OF ILLUSION *after* Alexis Michalik
KABUL GOES POP: MUSIC TELEVISION
　AFGHANISTAN
THE P WORD
THE REAL ONES

Annie Baker
THE ANTIPODES
THE FLICK
INFINITE LIFE
JOHN

Chris Bush
THE ASSASSINATION OF KATIE HOPKINS
　with Matt Winkworth
THE CHANGING ROOM
CHRIS BUSH PLAYS: ONE
A DOLL'S HOUSE *after* Ibsen
FAUSTUS: THAT DAMNED WOMAN
HUNGRY
JANE EYRE *after* Brontë
THE LAST NOËL
OTHERLAND
ROBIN HOOD AND THE CHRISTMAS
　HEIST *with* Matt Winkworth
ROCK / PAPER / SCISSORS
STANDING AT THE SKY'S EDGE
　with Richard Hawley
STEEL

Caryl Churchill
BLUE HEART
CHURCHILL PLAYS: THREE
CHURCHILL PLAYS: FOUR
CHURCHILL PLAYS: FIVE
CHURCHILL: SHORTS
CLOUD NINE
DING DONG THE WICKED
A DREAM PLAY *after* Strindberg
DRUNK ENOUGH TO SAY I LOVE YOU?
ESCAPED ALONE
FAR AWAY
GLASS. KILL. BLUEBEARD'S FRIENDS.
　IMP.
HERE WE GO
HOTEL
ICECREAM
LIGHT SHINING IN BUCKINGHAMSHIRE
LOVE AND INFORMATION
MAD FOREST
A NUMBER
PIGS AND DOGS
SEVEN JEWISH CHILDREN
THE SKRIKER
THIS IS A CHAIR
THYESTES *after* Seneca
TRAPS
WHAT IF IF ONLY

Natasha Gordon
NINE NIGHT

Dave Harris
TAMBO & BONES
TENDER

Branden Jacobs-Jenkins
APPROPRIATE
GLORIA
AN OCTOROON

Arinzé Kene
GOD'S PROPERTY
GOOD DOG
LITTLE BABY JESUS & ESTATE WALLS
MISTY

Lucy Kirkwood
BEAUTY AND THE BEAST
　with Katie Mitchell
BLOODY WIMMIN
THE CHILDREN
CHIMERICA
HEDDA *after* Ibsen
THE HUMAN BODY
IT FELT EMPTY WHEN THE HEART
　WENT AT FIRST BUT IT IS
　ALRIGHT NOW
LUCY KIRKWOOD PLAYS: ONE
MOSQUITOES
NSFW
RAPTURE
TINDERBOX
THE WELKIN

Chinonyerem Odimba
AMONGST THE REEDS
BLACK LOVE
PRINCESS & THE HUSTLER
UNKNOWN RIVERS

Ava Pickett
1536
EMMA *after* Austen
THE MANNINGTREE WITCHES
　after A. K. Blakemore

Lynn Nottage
CRUMBS FROM THE TABLE OF JOY
INTIMATE APPAREL
RUINED
SWEAT

Suzan-Lori Parks
FATHER COMES HOME FROM THE
　WARS (PARTS 1, 2 & 3)
RED LETTER PLAYS
TOPDOG/UNDERDOG

Margaret Perry
COLLAPSIBLE
PARADISE NOW!

Winsome Pinnock
LEAVE TAKING
PIG HEART BOY *after* Malorie Blackman
ROCKETS AND BLUE LIGHTS
TAKEN
TITUBA

debbie tucker green
BORN BAD
DEBBIE TUCKER GREEN PLAYS: ONE
DIRTY BUTTERFLY
EAR FOR EYE
HANG
NUT
A PROFOUNDLY AFFECTIONATE,
　PASSIONATE DEVOTION TO
　SOMEONE (– *NOUN*)
RANDOM
STONING MARY
TRADE & GENERATIONS
TRUTH AND RECONCILIATION

The Authenticator was first performed in the Dorfman auditorium of the National Theatre, London, on 2 April 2026. The cast, in alphabetical order, was as follows:

ABI	Rakie Ayola
FEN	Sylvestra Le Touzel
MARVA	Cherrelle Skeete
Director	Miranda Cromwell
Set Designer	Jon Bausor
Costume Designer	Kinnetia Isidore
Lighting Designer	Aideen Malone
Sound Designer	Tingying Dong
Composer	Benjamin Kwasi Burrell
Movement Director	Shelley Maxwell
Casting Director	Alastair Coomer CDG
Voice Coach	Hazel Holder
Staff Director	Dubheasa Lanipekun

Acknowledgements

The Authenticator was originally a seed commission for the Sphinx Theatre Lab.

Thanks and gratitude to Nancy Nordhoff (1932–2026) founder of Hedgebrook, Whidbey Island, Seattle. Thanks also to Nina Steiger, Kirsten Foster, Vivia Pinnock and Ayana Pinnock Johnson.

W.P.

Characters

FEN, *owner of Harford House*
MARVA, *an Authenticator*
ABI, *an Authenticator*

This text went to press before the end of rehearsals and so may differ slightly from the play as performed.

Scene One

The Small Library in Harford House.

FEN, *the owner of Harford House, shows* ABI *and her research assistant,* MARVA, *into the room. Six ancient leather-bound journals are laid out on a desk. Both* MARVA *and* ABI *are obviously delighted to see the artefacts.*

FEN. Here they are: all six of them. One for each year of his residence on the Jamaican farm.

MARVA. Did you really find them in a cardboard box?

FEN. When I was clearing out what my brother calls the Dungeon. Can you imagine?

MARVA. You had no idea that they existed before that?

FEN. Not a clue. I assume my brother had some hare-brained scheme for them that he never got round to executing.

ABI. You must have felt… How did you feel when you realised what they were?

FEN. It's impossible to put into words. You must get this all the time, when you handle historical documents.

MARVA. Handling documents in an archive is very different to discovering them in cardboard boxes in your family home.

FEN. I dare say it is. I was shocked and thrilled. As you say, it's not an everyday discovery.

FEN *puts on archival gloves; then, to* ABI*'s consternation, picks up one of the journals and riffles through its pages.*

They're actually rather beautiful objects, aren't they? His handwriting is meticulous.

Would you like a closer look? Oh.

FEN *takes off the gloves and hands them to* ABI.

MARVA. It's actually better to handle them without gloves.

FEN. Is it?

ABI. Gloves can damage the paper, Miss Harford.

FEN. James Warrener wore gloves when he handled them.

ABI. We can look at them from here, if you'd prefer?

FEN. No, no. And please call me Fen.

> MARVA *takes a furtive glance at* ABI *before eagerly taking the diary. She opens it carefully. She skim-reads the page she's on. She is immediately immersed.*

I'm afraid the contents are incredibly boring. Endless lists regarding the day-to-day running of the farm. If you want to know what the weather was like on any given day between 1756 and 1762, these diaries will tell you.

ABI. It might not read like Jane Austen but journals like these are incredible historical sources.

MARVA. You can say that again.

FEN (*to* MARVA). Found something interesting?

MARVA. He's made an inventory of his livestock. He lists people alongside pigs and cows.

FEN. I'm afraid I've only skimmed the first volume, so I don't really know what's in them.

MARVA. You always knew that a man who owned a farm in Jamaica in the eighteenth century was an enslaver though, right?

FEN. He was actually more known for his philanthropy. The Harford Foundation made huge donations to various abolitionist causes.

MARVA. I didn't know that Henry Harford was an abolitionist?

FEN. Not an abolitionist as such. But when he leased out the Jamaican farm and returned to England he was definitely a reformed man.

ABI. Like John Newton.

FEN. Sorry, who?

MARVA (*to* ABI). Volumes full of lists don't read like a Damascene conversion to me.

ABI (*to* FEN). Thank you for giving us this private view. We really appreciate it.

FEN. That's all down to Madge. Ever since we discovered the diaries she's been fielding requests to view them. Your letter stood out. Not least because we share a surname, but also because of your podcast where you said that your grandfather was an amateur historian with a special interest in Harford House.

ABI. It was my research assistant Doctor Harford – Marva – who actually wrote the letter. I am Doctor Adeyemi – Abi.

FEN. And a very good letter it was too.

MARVA. My grandfather loved English country houses. When I was a child we visited a different one every weekend, but this was his favourite.

FEN. How wonderful. And yours too?

MARVA. I can barely remember. I do remember that he said that your café did the best cream teas.

FEN. And does he still visit country houses?

MARVA *shakes her head.*

MARVA. He's no longer with us.

FEN. My sincere condolences.

MARVA. He went out to buy the *Daily Mirror* one morning and never came back. Vanished off the face of the earth.

FEN. That's terrible; not to know what happened to him.

MARVA. My condolences to you too. For your brother.

FEN. At least with my brother it was quick and decisive.

ABI. I'm so sorry.

FEN. We weren't that close considering we were twins.
(*To* MARVA.) Madge reckons his death was murder.

ABI. Really?

FEN. She thinks it was the house taking revenge on him for all the renovations. The reality is far more prosaic: my brother kept putting off getting the roof repaired until the inevitable happened. The primogenital order crushed by a pile of bricks. I'm the only Harford left standing.

MARVA. We're both orphans, then.

FEN. Are your parents gone as well?

MARVA *nods.*

MARVA. At least they have gravestones I can visit. Grandad disappeared without a trace.

FEN (*indicating the diaries*). Please don't stand on ceremony. Get stuck in.

ABI *picks up one of the journals and opens it.*

I couldn't understand half of it. It might as well have been written in another language, but I suppose you're used to that.

ABI. They do say that the past is another country.

MARVA. What are you going to do with them?

FEN. I haven't decided. Madge says the first step is to have them authenticated.

MARVA. I heard you'd asked James Warrener to do it.

FEN. How did you know that?

ABI. Our field is very niche. Word gets around. Professor Warrener is held in very high regard.

FEN. So I'm told.

MARVA. Just because Warrener's written loads of books on the subject doesn't mean he knows anything about enslavement.

FEN *and* ABI *look at* MARVA, *surprised.*

FEN. According to Professor Warrener, authentication is more a chemical process than one of historiography.

MARVA. That says it all.

ABI. It actually requires both.

MARVA. Warrener wrote an article called 'Burial Sites' where he goes on about how there are no graves of enslaved people to be found in Jamaica. If he'd talked to ordinary Jamaicans they'd have shown him the graves of their ancestors.

FEN. Are you saying that Warrener isn't a good choice?

MARVA. He's all right. But we'd be much better.

ABI (*embarrassed*). Ms Harford has already made her choice, Marva.

FEN. I haven't actually made a final decision.

ABI. I'm sorry about my colleague's bluntness.

Suddenly we hear rapid gunshots.

MARVA *and* ABI *drop to the ground.*

MARVA. What the fuck?

FEN (*amused*). Don't worry, they're just filming a music video.

We hear the sound of a driving bass, music.

ABI. I nearly had a heart attack

FEN. A grimy artist called Phallus-E.

MARVA (*pronounces it 'Fallacy'*). Phallus-E? I tried to book a ticket for his concert. I couldn't afford it.

FEN. You can watch Mister Phallus here for free.

MARVA *rushes to the window for a moment.*

MARVA. That's insane. He's all dressed up as an eighteenth-century dandy.

FEN. What does the E stand for?

MARVA. Edwin, or Edward.

FEN. Perhaps he should have just called himself Dickhead?

MARVA *laughs.*

MARVA. You're funny.

FEN. Does that surprise you?

MARVA. Yeah. I like it.

FEN *notices something out of the window.*

FEN. Oh God, he's in the fountain. I told them it was out of bounds. Excuse me.

FEN *makes a call on her mobile.*

Madge. They're in the fountain. Just tell them… Why not?

Frustrated, FEN *ends the call.*

I'll have to sort this out myself. Will you excuse me for one moment? I'll be right back.

FEN *goes.* ABI *and* MARVA *seem to breathe a sigh of relief.*

ABI. What's got into you?

MARVA. What? I'm just being myself.

ABI. You're showing off. I couldn't believe it when you said that we should do the authentication instead of Warrener.

MARVA. If you don't ask you don't get. And what about you? You've gone all speaky-spoky. 'What beautiful grounds.'

ABI. They *are* beautiful grounds. And I am always speaky-spoky as you put it.

MARVA. That was one of Grandad's words: speaky-spoky.

MARVA *is wandering round the room, looking at things, touching objects. She looks at a painting.*

ABI. Isn't that Thomas Vickery the abolitionist?

MARVA. I don't know. Is it?

ABI. What better way to rehabilitate yourself than to have your portrait painted with an abolitionist?

MARVA *picks up an ornament.*

Put that back, Marva. Don't touch anything.

MARVA *replaces the ornament.* ABI *walks around the table looking at the diaries.* MARVA *looks out of the window again.*

MARVA. My friends are going to go mad when I tell them that Phallus-E was here. (*Amused.*) Come and look. She's giving them all a right telling-off. What a character.

ABI. Your opinion, Doctor Harford. What's this cover made of?

MARVA *remains looking out of the window.*

MARVA. I'd say it was pure calfskin.

ABI. Very good. And who made these diaries?

MARVA. The Turkey Mill in Dorset.

ABI. You know that because…?

MARVA. There's a watermark on the front page.

ABI. Well done.

MARVA. I'm not being rude, Professor Adeyemi, but that's pretty basic stuff.

ABI. It may well be, but it's always a useful starting point. Why do you always call me Professor?

MARVA. If there was any justice in the world that's what you would be. What if she says yes?

ABI. She won't.

MARVA. You'd really be able to stick it to the Dean. He calls you into a meeting and says, 'I'm sorry but I'm going to have to give your department the chop,' but you go in and lick him with news that we are going to authenticate the newly discovered Harford Journals.

ABI. Experience tells me that hell would freeze over before she'd choose us over James Warrener.

They hear FEN *returning. They quickly gather themselves and affect to look at a painting in the room.*

FEN. So sorry about that.

MARVA. No problem. We were admiring this painting. Isn't that Thomas Vickery the abolitionist with Henry Harford?

FEN. Well spotted. By all accounts they were very close. Have you seen enough? Can I tempt you both to lunch? We have a new menu. (*To* MARVA.) You can tell me if it's as good as you remember?

ABI. We should be getting back. I have to attend a meeting with the Dean.

MARVA. I am feeling a bit peckish, though.

FEN. I'll get Madge to ask Chef to make you up a plate.

MARVA. And what about the authentication?

FEN. You're certainly much keener than Warrener was. And a lot more… animated.

MARVA. Warrener's got one foot in the grave. No wonder he's obsessed with burial sites.

ABI. Marva.

FEN. He was rather doddery. He kept going on about the difference between wood pulp and rag paper.

MARVA. We wouldn't do that. We'd just get on with it. I really think you should reconsider.

ABI. Please, Marva…

FEN. Why not? I've made up my mind. Why not?

ABI. Really? We'll have to get permission from the Dean.

MARVA. As if he's going to say no. We accept.

FEN. It'll be fun.

MARVA. Much more fun than Old Warrener.

FEN. I would rather the diaries not leave the premises so I suggest you stay here for the duration of the authentication.

ABI. Subject to the Dean's approval, of course.

MARVA. We'll have to set up a lab.

ABI. Nothing much. Just a computer and a few pieces of equipment.

FEN. Tell me what you need and I'll try to source it. I will talk to your Dean and we'll come to some agreement. I've got a good feeling about this. I'll get Madge to take you down to the restaurant. Welcome to Harford House.

MARVA and ABI wait for FEN to leave, then MARVA executes a little jig of victory. Holds up her hand for a high-five, which ABI reciprocates.

Scene Two

Morning. Three weeks later. The Small Library. ABI *and* MARVA *have set up a makeshift 'lab' which comprises a multi-screen computer and authentication equipment on the desk.* ABI *is taking off her outdoor coat and walking boots.*

ABI. I lost track of time. The quality of the light is different here, don't you think?

MARVA. Did you have that foot massage?

ABI. Just as well I did. I was walking for miles before I realised how far I'd gone. It was like walking on air. You should book a treatment.

MARVA. Spas aren't my thing.

ABI. Your generation thrives on the stress of confrontation. Trust me, it will take its toll one day. (*Stretches her arms out.*) Aren't we so lucky? I was worried that the Dean wouldn't release us.

MARVA. I knew he would. We're his blue-eyed girls. In a manner of speaking.

ABI. He said he didn't know how we pulled it off. 'Pulled it off.' As though this was some kind of heist.

MARVA. In his mind it probably is. He's plotting how to claim ownership of the authentication as we speak.

ABI *looks at* MARVA*'s notes over her shoulder.*

ABI. What have we got to?

MARVA. The ink tests were all fine, although there were mismatches across the different volumes. But that's in keeping with the fact that Harford had supplies shipped from England at different times. He was very particular about his materials. Once he found something he liked, he stuck with it.

ABI. The punctiliousness of enslavers never fails to amaze me. Any anomalies?

MARVA. A couple.

ABI. Only two?

MARVA. There's a page missing from volume three.

ABI. There are always pages missing.

MARVA. It looks as though it has been torn out. Shall I make a note of it? I'm going to make a note of it.

ABI (*approving*). Good.

Slight pause.

We record everything because…?

MARVA. We need to create an accurate description of the artefact.

ABI. What's the other anomaly? You said there were two.

MARVA. This one's more interesting. On the tenth of April 1759, Harford records that his wife Hannah gave birth to a stillborn.

ABI. Poor woman.

MARVA *searches the volume for the page.*

MARVA (*reading*). 'Firstborn son died.' That's the only time he mentions it. However, a few months later he and Hannah attend a luncheon given by their neighbour Lucy Johnson. And when I cross-reference her diaries… she mentions the Harfords attending with their baby.

ABI *isn't expecting that.*

ABI. That is interesting.

MARVA. The baptismal records for that year record the Harfords' registration of the birth. Why did he write that the baby died if it lived?

ABI (*thinking on her feet*). It wasn't unusual for a baby to be born not breathing. The midwife would have given it the kiss of life.

MARVA. Or they could have had twins – twins run in their family – one died and one lived.

There is a knock at the door.

ABI. Harford recorded the death of a piglet: he would have recorded his child's burial.

MARVA. You're right. The baby lived. I'll make a note of it.

FEN *enters holding a tea tray.*

FEN. Don't you ever take a break? You must be starving.

ABI. That looks wonderful, but I'm still stuffed from breakfast.

FEN. The brain requires nourishment. I'm just as bad, I haven't sat down all day. Just as I think everything is organised, something goes kaput. Horrendous. However, the electrician has installed a new generator in the Dungeon. And we shall have light for our Festival of Light. (*To* MARVA.) Tuck in. The lemon drizzle cake is for you. You seemed particularly fond of it last time. I haven't forgotten that I promised you a tour of the house.

ABI (*to* FEN). Thank you. Your festival sounds lovely.

FEN. It has been the highlight of village life for many years. And it is lovely. Until it descends into Bacchanalian debauchery, which it does every single year.

MARVA. Mmmmm.

She gives a thumbs-up.

FEN. I'll take you on the tour after lunch. Is that all right?

ABI. Honestly, there's no need. You sound incredibly busy.

FEN. It will be good practice for me. My brother took great pride in his tours and he's a tough act to follow.

ABI. That's very kind of you.

FEN. How's it going?

ABI. The main challenge so far is that Harford wrote so much.

MARVA. And yet so little.

ABI. You weren't exaggerating when you said he recorded everything.

MARVA. Yet nothing that you really want to know.

FEN. Such as?

MARVA. His thoughts, his feelings, his interior life.

ABI. It's not a novel, Marva.

FEN. I don't know how you manage to wade through it all. I was stumped after the first few pages. It might as well be written in another language. I bought your book, by the way.

ABI. That was written in English.

FEN. I didn't mean –

ABI. I'm impressed that you got hold of it. It's out of print.

FEN. Madge can get hold of anything. I'm looking forward to reading it.

MARVA. I wouldn't. It's a bit dry.

ABI jokingly 'smacks' MARVA on the back of the head.

ABI. What she means is that it's written for academics.

FEN. I'm sure it's compelling.

MARVA. It isn't.

FEN. I'll come back and fetch you. For the tour.

ABI. We have met before, you know.

FEN. Have we?

ABI. We were at Oxford at the same time. We played the Jericho Tavern on the same night.

MARVA. You're kidding.

FEN. Everyone at the art school was in a band.

ABI. You had green hair.

FEN. And jet-black and purple hair. That was another life. We put away childish things, and here we are. I shall wrap up with the engineer and come and find you in – what? – half an hour?

FEN goes.

MARVA. You didn't say you were in a band?

ABI. She had a cockney accent in those days.

MARVA. No way.

ABI. We all reinvented ourselves at university.

MARVA. Some of us don't have to. You're a dark horse, Doctor Adeyemi.

ABI. That's enough of that. Back to work.

MARVA raises a toast with cake then stuffs it into her mouth and eats. They get back to work.

Scene Three

Later the same day. This scene comprises a montage of scenes in various locations around the house. I imagine that the realism of the early scenes gives way to a more imaginative space, with very quick transitions from one imagined location to another.

FEN *gives* MARVA *and* ABI *the Harford House tour. She is showing them the fireplace.*

FEN. The Rose Chamber where, according to family folklore, Queen Victoria stayed during a secret visit. She is said to have appreciated the aroma of roses which wafts up from the garden.

ABI. Mmm. I can smell the roses.

FEN (*referring to the fireplace*). The rose theme is echoed in the intricate carvings. And for those of you who are fans of *The Parlourmaid*, this is the very fireplace in front of which Lord Halliwell seduced Imogen Bloom.

ABI. Is it? That's amazing. I thought this room seemed familiar.

MARVA (*surprised, to* ABI). Don't tell me you watch *The Parlourmaid*.

ABI. It's incredibly relaxing.

FEN. Every time it airs our bookings shoot up. This chamber was added to the house when Henry Harford undertook the refurbishment in around 1840.

ABI. Which Harford are we talking about?

MARVA. The grandson of the author of our journals.

FEN. If it helps we could call him Henry the Third.

MARVA. The property was first purchased by Henry the First. The author of the journals.

FEN. In around 1763, when he left the Jamaican farm in the care of overseers…

MARVA. After Tacky's rebellion.

FEN. …and came back to England.

MARVA. With Hannah and their son Henry the Second.

FEN. That's right.

ABI. That's a lot of Henrys.

FEN. Every firstborn son is named Henry. I'm the first and will probably be the last owner who isn't so named. Let's go through this door here…

FEN disappears through a door and appears in a different part of the stage.

MARVA and ABI hang back.

MARVA (*teasing* ABI *with her play-acting*). Lady Bloom, I am going to put flower petals all over you and ravish you. Right here. Now. In front of this blazing fireplace.

ABI. Very funny.

MARVA. I'm learning quite a lot about you on this trip. I would never have guessed that you watch *The Parlourmaid*.

ABI. Don't you dare tell anyone.

MARVA. We all have our secret passions. I bet these walls have been privy to a few secrets. Imagine how much tea they'd have to spill if only they could talk.

ABI. They certainly would. If *The Parlourmaid* is anything to go by.

MARVA. They paid for this refurbishment with the money they were given in compensation for the loss of enslaved labour after abolition. Several million in today's money.

ABI. Talk about coming up smelling of roses.

FEN (*offstage*). Are you with me?

ABI. Where did she go?

MARVA. Through here, I think.

ABI. We'd better catch her up.

MARVA goes out of the door and joins FEN. ABI hangs around and looks around the room. Takes a deep breath in.

Roses.

MARVA puts her head round the door.

MARVA. Come on, Abi. Chop-chop

   MARVA *disappears.* ABI *joins her.*

* * *

The Large Study.

FEN. This is the Large Study.

MARVA. It's smaller than the Small Study.

FEN. He had a sense of humour.

ABI. What does that ceiling remind me of?

FEN. The Sistine Chapel?

ABI. Oh yes.

FEN. Whenever he needed to escape he could just come in here and look up at the ceiling.

ABI. And be transported to Rome.

FEN. Quite.

MARVA. I've never been to Rome. Or Venice.

ABI. We'll have to take you.

   ABI *approaches a painting.*

   Is this a Gainsborough?

   MARVA *is leaning against a wall and is shocked when it swings inwards and she disappears through a secret door – unseen by the others.*

FEN. It's by a minor artist who aspired to Gainsborough's genius. It is an exact representation of this room. A picture within a picture.

ABI. Like a hall of mirrors.

FEN. We try to keep the room exactly as they have it in the painting. The chessboard is original but most of the other objects are reproductions.

ABI. I wonder who the black boy is.

FEN. Which black boy?

   ABI *points him out to* FEN.

ABI. There.

> MARVA *re-enters through the secret door, brandishing a sword and wearing the helmet from a suit of armour. She stands behind* FEN *and* ABI, *looking at the painting.*

FEN. Oh, yes.

> FEN *takes a closer look.*

I've never noticed him before.

ABI. You can't miss him.

FEN. He's very well dressed, isn't he? We'll have to look into it.

MARVA. That's not a boy. It's a statue.

ABI. You're right. It's one of those so-called blackamoor statues.

FEN. Of course. He was stood in that corner for ages. But after the George Floyd affair a couple of visitors complained so we got rid of him.

MARVA. Quite right too.

> ABI *clocks* MARVA*'s helmet and does a double-take.*

FEN. We banished him to the Dungeon. (*Referring to* MARVA*'s sword.*) You've discovered the hidden door?

> MARVA *takes off the helmet and brandishes the sword.*

MARVA. This is so fucking cool. En garde.

ABI. You'll have someone's head off with that.

FEN. It was my favourite hiding place when we played hide-and-seek.

> FEN *takes the sword from* MARVA.

It was left behind by one of the film crews. They'll be coming back for it at some point, so I'd better put it back.

> FEN *disappears through the hidden door. While she is gone,* ABI *and* MARVA *wander around the room looking at paintings, objects.*

ABI. Every room is more beautiful than the last. Can you imagine what it was like to grow up here?

MARVA. You'd have to be careful that you didn't break anything. No wonder people like that are so... stiff.

ABI. Look at the view from that window. If that isn't freedom, I don't know what is.

MARVA. As Bob Marley says: freedom is a state of mind.

MARVA *looks at the painting.*

ABI. And those incredible horses. I haven't ridden since I was a child.

MARVA. Only thing I've ever ridden is the seventy-three bus to Stokey.

ABI *looks at the painting again.*

ABI. Thomas Vickery looks so pleased with himself.

MARVA. He should be. He's nabbed himself an enslaver.

ABI. Reformed enslaver.

MARVA. Isn't that an oxymoron?

ABI. That statue does look like a real person, doesn't it?

FEN *appears in the doorway.*

FEN. I'll take you to the Dungeon, shall I? That's great fun. Follow me.

FEN *leaves.* ABI *and* MARVA *take a final look at the painting then follow her.*

* * *

The Dungeon.

Darkness. FEN *shines a torch and walks ahead of* ABI *and* MARVA.

FEN. Welcome to the Dungeon.

MARVA. Can we have a light on? I can't see my own hand.

FEN. My brother thought that candles made it more atmospheric.

MARVA. What do you do with a dungeon in this day and age?

FEN. His Haunted House tour was very popular, although not as lucrative as he'd imagined.

MARVA. Something's just touched me.

ABI. Give over, Marva.

MARVA. Whatever it was just scuttled away.

FEN. We had pest control in just a few days ago.

> FEN *shines the torch in* MARVA*'s direction.* ABI *screams as she glimpses the blackamoor statue standing behind* MARVA. MARVA *screams too, although she doesn't know why. She turns and sees the statue and screams again.*

ABI. Oh my God.

FEN. It's just a statue.

MARVA. That gave me a scare.

FEN. It's only Melvin.

MARVA. Melvin?

FEN. We're keeping him down here until we decide what to do with him.

MARVA. Why Melvin?

FEN. That was my father's name for him.

> FEN *talks to 'Melvin'.*

You are so handsome, aren't you. Melly? Imagine having to banish him to the Dungeon. He used to serve as a waiter at dinner parties. Papa used to say he was better value for money than the rest of his staff put together.

MARVA. You shouldn't touch his face like that. It's disrespectful.

FEN. It's just a statue.

ABI. Blackamoor statues were modelled after real enslaved people.

FEN. Really?

We suddenly hear the sound of ghostly sobs.

MARVA. Someone's hurt themself.

VOICE. Help. Somebody, help me, please.

Pause.

FEN *laughs.*

SCENE THREE 27

FEN. Don't be alarmed. It's just part of my brother's tour.

VOICE. I am the Runaway Bride. Trapped within the walls of the Dungeon for all eternity.

FEN takes out a remote control and turns down the volume of the recording, which continues to tell its story.

FEN. My brother loved gimmicks like this. So does the public. I'm sorry if I scared you. I didn't mean to. Perhaps this will help to calm you down.

FEN produces a couple of bottles of wine.

When he wasn't scaring people in it, my brother used it to store his wine. We can have these with dinner. My treat after scaring you half to death.

The lights go on. We can see some of Fen's artist's paraphernalia and a couple of boxes full of tat.

ABI. You've started a new sculpture? That's exciting.

FEN. I have a desire, but I'm not yet sure of its object.

ABI. You're blocked?

FEN. Having to run this place doesn't help. I don't know if I'll ever get that side of myself back again.

ABI. Are these the boxes where you found the diaries?

FEN. I live in hope of finding another treasure, but there's been nothing so far.

Suddenly there is a banging on the wall.

That's not me.

A different kind of wailing is heard, more poignant and haunting, followed by a banging sound.

MARVA. What the hell is it?

FEN. Ancient plumbing, structural shifts.

Suddenly there is a loud creaking or tearing sound.

ABI. Goodness, it sounds as though the whole thing's about to come crashing down.

FEN. The surveyor assures me that the foundations are firm.

The wailing sound again.

ABI. It sounds as though it's trying to tell us something.

The sound stops. The lights go up.

FEN. And that's the end of the Haunted House part of the tour.

ABI. There's more?

FEN. You deserve some fresh air after this dingy old dungeon. To our final destination, the Maze.

ABI. Are you okay? You look ashen.

MARVA. There's something I… I'll tell you later.

ABI. What is it?

MARVA. Later. Let's get this over with.

They follow FEN *to the Maze.*

* * *

The Maze.

MARVA *and* ABI *wander around different parts of the Maze. They can't see each other.*

FEN. The Harford Hedge Maze wasn't added to the house until 1925. At the centre of every maze resides the man-eating monster, the Minotaur.

Beat.

King Minos set a challenge for his subjects to destroy the monster.

MARVA. How do we get out of here?

ABI. I'm back where I started.

MARVA. I'm looking at a dead end.

FEN. Follow my voice. Both of you. Theseus wanted to win the challenge so that he could also win the hand of Minos's daughter. Can you hear me? The daughter provided him with a map so that he wasn't confused by the twists and turns of the labyrinth.

They both follow her voice and reach an impasse.

ABI. I've reached a dead end.

MARVA. The hedges are growing. They're closing in on me.

ABI. She's having a panic attack. I'm coming, Marva.

But ABI *can't go anywhere because she's reached a dead end.*
MARVA *gasps for breath. She is having a panic attack.*

FEN. It is those twists and turns which defeat the Minotaur's challengers.

ABI. What did you say? I can't hear you.

MARVA. Get me out.

FEN. Put your dominant hand against the hedge and keep it on the hedge as you keep walking. Whatever you do don't take your hand off the hedge.

ABI. Relax, Marva. Imagine you're breathing into a paper bag.

ABI *and* MARVA *put their hands out and follow the hedge, taking a twisting and turning path as* FEN *speaks.*

FEN. Theseus had a map and therefore gained an advantage over the Minotaur, swiftly slaying the monster and finding his way out of the maze using the map given to him by his beloved.

ABI *and* MARVA *have made it out of the Maze.*

See, there was nothing to it. You can't get lost in a maze. Is she all right?

MARVA *sits on the ground, breathing heavily.*

ABI. Deep breaths, Marva, deep breaths – deep breaths.

FEN. Shall I call an ambulance?

ABI. Breathe, Marva, breathe. (*To* FEN.) It looks worse than it is.

MARVA*'s breathing has returned to normal.*

You had us worried for a minute there.

MARVA. I'm all right now.

FEN. Perhaps this is a good time to go and meet the horses?

MARVA. My grandad's name was Melvin.

Slight pause.

FEN. Really?

MARVA. Why did you name the statue after my grandfather?

FEN. Was your grandfather an electrician? Our Melvin was named after a rather dodgy electrician who did some work for the Festival of Lights. He wasn't very good: the lights went pop just as things were heating up.

MARVA. He was a bus driver. But he used to be an electrician.

FEN. Our man scarpered pretty quick after the lights went out. I'm guessing your grandfather wasn't a bolter.

MARVA. It's just when you mentioned his name...

ABI. I can see why you're shaken. Who wouldn't be?

FEN. Shall we go to the stables? The horses will calm us down.

MARVA. I'll sit this out if you don't mind.

ABI. Do you want me to stay with you?

MARVA. No, please, you go, Abi.

ABI. Are you sure?

MARVA. I'll see you both at dinner. I need to lie down.

ABI. That sounds like a good idea. You rest, Marva.

MARVA *leaves.*

What are the odds of that?

FEN. It can't be the same man, surely?

ABI. The older I get the more I realise that the world is infinitesimally small.

FEN. Isn't it just? Come on, the horses will restore our equanimity.

Scene Four

The Small Library.

ABI *is standing in the doorway with her back to us. She wears jeans and a jumper. She is looking out into the countryside beyond.* MARVA *is sitting reading one of the journals.*

ABI. Did you see me galloping across the field? It's so… bracing. The horse she gave me was powerful. Sensitive too. They pick up on your every emotion, you know.

ABI *moves into the room.*

I'm going to teach you to ride. I know some stables in London. You'll be grateful to me forever. It's the closest we'll ever get to flying. I want you to experience that. Have you been sat here all afternoon?

MARVA. Grandad used to write letters to Fen's father.

ABI. Did he? What sort of letters?

MARVA. He believed he was a blood descendant of the Harfords. Everyone thought he was crazy. He wrote these letters claiming a stake in Harford House. My grandmother tried to stop him, but he just kept writing the letters. In the end the Harfords' solicitor sent him a cease and desist letter. He'd never had anything to do with the law before. He was humiliated. He was never the same after that.

ABI. I had no idea.

MARVA. I wish I'd listened to what he was telling me, but Little Miss Know-It-All here just had to put him straight and tell him that it was common for enslaved families to take the names of the enslavers, that it didn't prove any blood relation.

ABI. You were right to remind him of that because it's true.

MARVA. Maybe I should have taken him more seriously.

ABI. How would he prove that you were blood relatives and what would be gained if he did? Enslaved people had no legal right to property.

MARVA. He didn't just make it all up. The idea was passed down through the family by word of mouth for generations.

ABI. He was quite ill at the end though, wasn't he?

MARVA. Even though he had Alzheimer's, I swear, Abi, there were moments when his mind was razor-sharp.

Slight pause.

I should have paid attention. When he'd bring me here he'd sneak beyond the silken rope into one of these forbidden rooms. It was like a secret mission. He kept touching things, looking at objects as though he was looking for something. What was he looking for?

ABI. Are you sure that's what he was doing?

MARVA. He was either looking for something or trying to leave some trace of himself behind.

ABI *suddenly realises something.*

ABI. You didn't request that we get this job so that you could fulfill your grandfather's design, did you?

MARVA. Of course not. I wasn't to know that they named a blackamoor statue after my grandfather. Had him standing in the corner like a servant, serving drinks to their guests.

ABI. We're supposed to declare conflicts of interest. I'll have to inform the Dean.

MARVA. Please don't do that, Abi. He'll have us taken off the authentication. The department will go under. You'd never be able to live with yourself.

ABI *sighs. She knows that* MARVA *is right.*

ABI. I want you to promise that you're not going to treat this like some kind of historical detective quest.

MARVA. I promise.

ABI. Our role here is to authenticate. Nothing more.

MARVA. I've done a good job so far, haven't I?

ABI. You've been brilliant. And I want you to go on being brilliant.

Save the detective work for when we've finished. You can put it in your podcast.

Slight pause.

We've got a bit of time before Fen's dinner. I'm going to start my report.

ABI *sits at her desk.* MARVA *sits at hers.*

MARVA. I think I'll give dinner a miss. I'm not feeling up to it.

ABI. Fine. I'll give Fen your apologies.

They both get their heads down and work.

MARVA. I found another anomaly.

ABI. Mmmm?

MARVA. Fen said the diaries were all lists and inventories but he does have the odd outburst where he writes prose.

ABI. Does he?

MARVA. He's obsessed with this woman, Black Sarah.

ABI. Black Sarah?

MARVA. She was one of the enslaved women who worked on the farm.

MARVA *picks up the diary.*

(*Reading from the diary.*) Seventeenth of June 1759. 'I look up from writing and am surprised to catch the mulatto woman, Black Sarah's stare and I am the devil himself. She catches wind of my sighting and performs an insouciant deference. I send her to the Summerhouse.'

ABI. I was hoping the journals really were just lists and inventories, but they never are, are they?

MARVA. He sends her to the 'Summerhouse'. You know what that means, don't you?

ABI. I know what it means.

MARVA. You can feel her rage. He feels it too. He sends her to the outhouse where he metes out his punishment. See these notches? Each notch represents five lashes. Ten lashes. And here and here. So far he's mentioned her eight times. Here, read.

ABI. I don't want to.

MARVA. Why not?

ABI. I know what happens in the 'Summerhouse'. I know this story. I don't have to read it.

MARVA. That's the difference between us. I'm compelled to keep reading because this isn't just a story for me, is it? This isn't just history. This is me.

ABI. You just promised that you'd focus on the authentication.

MARVA. Don't worry, Abi. I won't let you down. I can pretend that this has nothing to do with me. I can switch off all emotion and maintain the utmost professionalism, conduct the chemical tests, undertake all the searches without shedding a single tear for Black Sarah. Just like you taught me.

MARVA goes.

ABI. Marva, wait.

ABI leaves. Silence. The pages of the journal flutter open as though blown by the wind.

FEN appears through the hidden door, carrying the costume MARVA found earlier. She allows it to fall to the floor. She picks up the diary, and looks for a page.

FEN. Seventeenth of June.

FEN reads. Her face dissolves in a similar horror to ABI's earlier.

(*Reading.*) ...Five, ten, fifteen, twenty...

She mutters under her breath.

She is suddenly unable to handle the diary, as though it is burning hot. She paces the room, distraught, stands in front of the painting.

Black Sarah.

FEN leaves the room.

Scene Five

The Dungeon.

Later that night. FEN *and* ABI *are both sitting on the floor of the Dungeon trying to pretend that they're not drunk. A couple of empty bottles are strewn on the floor. The signs of work in progress.* FEN *is in the middle of giving a drunken rendition of a punk song.*

FEN.
   You said I should come
   When I came you weren't there
   You promised me love
   But you just didn't care
   Sick of your lies
   The contempt in your eyes
   As you prowl the streets out on the hunt
   Free for today
   I refuse to be prey
   So see you next Tuesday
   Yer cunt
   See you next Tuesday
   Yer cunt.

   ABI *claps and cheers.*

   Your turn.

ABI. I'm not a singer.

FEN. Just a flavour of it. I want to hear this Fanon.

ABI. We took his brilliant prose, cut it up...

FEN. Sing me one of his songs.

ABI. Called ourselves The Wretched of the Earth.

FEN. Why do the young have to be so negative? Sing.

ABI. I'm naked without my djembe.

FEN. Improvise. Here...

   FEN *beats out a rhythm on the floor.* ABI *corrects the rhythm to a slower pace.* FEN *picks up* ABI*'s rhythm.*

   What a depressing beat.

ABI *coughs in preparation.*

FEN *nods encouragement.*

ABI *sings. The song is plaintive, haunting.*

ABI (*singing*).
You are born anywhere
You die anywhere
Hungry for bread, for shoes and for light
People piled on people
No space
No Space
People piled on people
No space
No Space.

Pause.

FEN. That's very moving.

ABI. We converted a lot of students with that song.

FEN. Sign me up. I'm in.

They both laugh.

ABI. That was a wonderful dinner, Fen. And the wine…

FEN. The new chef is a genius, isn't she?

ABI. I'm stuffed.

Pause.

Horses are amazing… You wonder why they let us ride them. What made you choose Midnight for me?

FEN. You enjoyed each other, didn't you?

ABI. But why the black horse?

Pause.

FEN. Is this another *Confrontation with Whiteness*?

ABI *laughs.*

ABI. Nobody actually ever reads that book, you know.

FEN. I read the conclusion.

SCENE FIVE 37

ABI. Very wise. And what do you mean 'another' *Confrontation with Whiteness*?

FEN. I'm feeling rather… attacked at the moment.

ABI. Who's attacking you?

FEN. You don't like me very much, do you?

ABI. Where's this coming from?

FEN. I give you the run of the house, a nice dinner, and you and Marva still hate me.

ABI. We don't hate you.

FEN. Why not? You should, shouldn't you? After everything Henry Harford…

ABI. I think I'll call it a day.

FEN. It's too early to go to bed.

ABI. If I stay I'll just keep drinking that wonderful wine. I'll end up talking shit like you.

FEN tries to get up and finds that she can't. She flops back onto the floor.

ABI flops back onto the floor.

Both women seem to be floating on the ground.

The floor's all… fluid.

FEN. 'History should help us shape the future, but should not determine our present subjectivities.' What does that even mean?

ABI. My argument… my argument is that if we identify ourselves too closely with trauma we risk perpetuating our own mental enslavement.

FEN. We have a lot in common, you and I.

ABI. Because we both went to Oxford?

FEN. We are both descended from families that profited from the slave trade.

ABI sits up, suddenly sober.

ABI. What my ancestors did was very different to the chattel slavery practised by your forebears. The enslaved were free to live amongst the group, even marry into it.

FEN. They were free?

ABI. Within certain parameters, yes.

Pause.

FEN. In your book you say that *your* forebears facilitated the European trade in slaves –

ABI (*correcting her*). Enslaved people.

FEN. Enslaved, yes. Do you carry their shame?

ABI. The book is not a mea culpa. I am not responsible for their actions. What I do with the legacy of their actions? That's my responsibility.

FEN. What do you do with the legacy?

ABI. I… I… I run a scheme for young people from deprived homes and help them to prepare for university from primary school onwards. Marva was my first success story. And probably my last. Like everything else these days, the future of the charity is hanging by a thread.

Pause.

FEN. You feel compelled to repair the damage done to Marva by your ancestors.

ABI. She may bear the legacy of a damaged history, but Marva is not damaged.

FEN. I think she's a wonderful girl, a force of nature.

ABI. That sounds patronising.

FEN. Like you, I would love to help her.

Pause.

ABI. Do you know how you can help Marva and others like her? By giving up your power and privilege.

FEN. Power. What power do I have?

ABI *blurts out a laugh of disbelief.*

ABI. This looks like power to me.

FEN. You're from an elite Nigerian family. Are you going to give up your privilege?

ABI. This isn't about me or my ancestors. It's about you and yours.

FEN. You more than anyone understand the significance of legacy. Yet you ask me to give it up?

ABI. Over your dead body, eh?

FEN. Whatever we think of him, Henry Harford made a huge contribution to this community.

ABI. How many black people have profited from his largesse? Come on, how many?

FEN. How the hell should I know that?

ABI. I bet there hasn't been a single one.

Pause.

FEN. If you want a donation for your scheme, you are welcome to apply to the foundation...

ABI. Did I say I wanted your money?

FEN. It was just a suggestion.

Pause.

When the responsibility of running Harford House fell on my shoulders, I was suddenly confronted with the enormity of something built up and preserved by my family over centuries.

ABI. You're as inured to the idea that this belongs to you as any other aristocrat.

FEN. Unlike you, I am not from a royal line. Henry Harford left England with nothing but the clothes on his back.

ABI. And being a white man in Jamaica, albeit a nobody, he was able to accrue a fortune in just a few years.

FEN. What do you want from me? You want me to rectify what he did? I'll do it. I'll give you what you want.

FEN *stands.*

I, Fenella Eugenia Harford, bequeath all of my estate, real, personal, tangible and intangible, wherever stated, to Doctor Marva Harford.

FEN *gives her head a wobble as though trying to shake herself sober.*

You are a witness to that.

ABI. The only authentic promise is one that's written down. But you know that, don't you?

FEN. Why should I have to take responsibility for a crime when I am no guiltier than you are?

ABI *laughs.*

ABI. Not guilty, your honour.

FEN. Stop coming for me.

ABI. How am I coming for you? That's your guilty conscience speaking.

Slight pause. Both women sway. They hold on to each other to steady themselves. They let go.

FEN. You're drunk.

ABI. I do have a bone to pick with you.

FEN. Pick away.

ABI. At Oxford. You never once acknowledged me. Not once. Did you even see me?

FEN. It was a long time ago.

ABI. You don't remember me. I might as well have been invisible to you.

FEN. I refuse to be what you seem hell-bent on making me into.

ABI. What happened to your cockney accent, eh, Fen? (*Cockney accent.*) Lost it, 'ave yer. You poor little rich girl.

ABI *laughs.*

FEN, *drunk and furious, contemplates* ABI *for a moment, but is too drunk to do or say anything.* ABI *laughs to herself and goes.*

FEN (*cockney accent*). Fuck you.

FEN *goes.*

Scene Six

Late that night. MARVA *is recording her podcast. The sound travels through gratings to* FEN, *who is listening. She is wearing a leather jacket. She puts gel in her hair, styling it into a Mohican. Every now and then she takes angry swigs from a bottle.*

MARVA (*recorded*). If we take one element of the gothic novel – the secret passage, for example – it's not difficult to see what it represents: a journey into the darkest recesses of the collective subconscious.

The secret passage leads to a dungeon and hidden there is a creature imprisoned by the powerful owners of the country house. She threatens to overturn that power because more often than not the creature is the rightful owner of the property, tricked out of it by the deception of the owners.

FEN *drains the bottle and throws it away. She picks up another bottle and takes it with her as she leaves the room.*

Scene Seven

The Small Library.

MARVA *and* FEN *tumble into the room.* FEN *has a wine bottle and a glass in hand.* MARVA *wears pyjamas and a dressing gown, and carries a washbag. She can't stop staring at* FEN*'s Mohican, leather jacket and unevenly applied eyeliner.*

FEN. I am so glad I caught you.

MARVA. I was just about to go to bed.

FEN. You must have a nightcap.

She gives MARVA *the glass and fills it with wine, indicates for* MARVA *to sit.*

You missed a rather wonderful dinner, but I didn't want you to miss out on this… it is very old and very beautiful. Imbibe. Savour it. Relax.

MARVA *drinks.* FEN *watches as* MARVA*'s face indicates that the wine is indeed beautiful. Through the scene* FEN *keeps refilling* MARVA*'s glass.*

I hate the thought that my family was involved in this awful business. I speak for all Harfords when I say that we are very very sorry. Thank God it is all in the past. And it will never happen again.

MARVA. No offence, Fen, but you stink of alcohol.

FEN. I knew you would understand. You understand what it's like to be an outsider.

MARVA. How are you an outsider?

FEN. All women are outsiders.

Slight pause.

Papa was always taking my brother off for cosy little secret chats mano-a-mano. I followed them once, tracked them through the Maze by following their voices, but they must have caught wind of me and started talking in whispers. I lost them. (*Conspiratorial.*) I have something to tell you. In confidence.

FEN *beckons* MARVA *closer.*

This house is full of secrets. Every object in it is weighted with a meaning that I have never been able to work out. They keep it all to themselves, these Harford men; passing their secrets down to each other for generations. You know what I'm saying, don't you?

MARVA. Maybe…

FEN. You and me, we're both trying to find our way out of the dark. We are both searching for…

MARVA. Searching for…?

SCENE SEVEN 43

FEN. What they don't want us to know. What was your grandfather searching for?

MARVA. Searching for?

FEN. When he took you around the house and touched all the objects.

MARVA. Were you eavesdropping on my conversation with Abi?

FEN. Of course not. The sound carries in this house. That's the way it's designed. Like an early telephone system.

MARVA *pours herself a drink from the bottle.*

MARVA. Do you know where my grandfather's letters are?

FEN. I don't know anything about your grandfather's letters. They probably threw them away. My brother was going to throw the diaries away, you know.

MARVA. That doesn't surprise me.

FEN. But I rescued them. Me. I would have done the same with your letters if I'd seen them because I am not afraid of the truth.

Slight pause.

Everybody who grows up in a house like this knows it, but they'll swear blind that a painting is just a painting. But you and I know different, don't we?

MARVA. If a painting isn't just a painting, what is it?

FEN. Every object in this house is loaded with meaning. A meaning that even I don't understand.

MARVA. They didn't throw away the diaries, so they may not have thrown away my grandfather's letters. They may be hidden at the back of a desk or something.

FEN. That's a possibility.

MARVA. I want to find them, Fen. I want to know what he wrote. Will you help me find them?

FEN. I'll help you. Right now. I'll help you.

MARVA. Right now?

FEN. There's no point in wasting time. We'll do it now. Right now. I want to help you, Marva.

MARVA. Okay. Okay. Let's do it now.

Neither is quite sure what to do. FEN *pours them both another drink.*

Scene Eight

The Small Library.

ABI *swigs from the bottle as she looks at the diary on the table. She seems to be trying to make her mind up about something. She puts the bottle down and picks up the diary, quickly turns to the page from earlier and reads.*

ABI. 'June seventeenth… mmmm… Black Sarah… mmmm… Summerhouse…'

She shakes her head.

Of course I know what happens in the Summerhouse.

She closes the book.

I can't. Not today. I must.

She continues reading.

…Five, ten, fifteen…

ABI *quickly turns the page and leaves her hand on it. She closes her eyes.*

Poor Black Sarah. Sarah. Sarah…

As she intones Sarah's name, she lightly rubs her hand over the page. Soon she is aware that she can feel something…

Indentations?

ABI *continues to run her hands over the page.*

Like Braille. A message?

ABI *quickly gets up, excitedly searches for something on the table.*

Tracing paper. Tracing paper. Pencil.

She fetches the objects. She places the tracing paper over the page of the journal, then lightly rubs over the surface of the paper. What she sees (which we the audience can't, of course) is the marks of writing revealed.

Like magic…

ABI *lifts the tracing paper from the journal and holds it to the light. She tries to read it.*

The missing entry… (*Shocked.*) I've found it. The missing page.

ABI *is so overjoyed and excited that she does a little dance of joy.*

I've found you, Black Sarah. I've found you.

Scene Nine

The Large Study.

A Chesterfield armchair has its stuffing pulled out. Drawers in desks are pulled out. The painting of Harford has been taken down from the wall. FEN *has a hammer in her hand as she looks at Harford's portrait.* MARVA *is now is as drunk as* FEN. MARVA *opens the chessboard and looks inside.*

FEN. The letters might be hidden in here. You know, like drug traffickers do with cocaine.

MARVA. I suppose you know how their minds work.

FEN. Anything?

  MARVA *shrugs. Closes the chessboard.*

MARVA. Let's call it a night. We've looked everywhere.

FEN (*to picture of Harford*). What are you looking at, eh?

MARVA. He's looking at me. His eyes keep following me around the room.

MARVA *moves away from the chessboard but is aware that Harford's eyes are following her around the room.*

Why's he looking at me like that?

FEN (*to Harford*). Stop looking at her. I said stop looking at her.

FEN *moves towards the painting, hammer in hand.*

MARVA. Don't, Fen. You'll damage the...

But FEN *is fetching blows to the picture frame with the hammer.*

FEN. Filthy stinking pervert.

FEN *hands* MARVA *the hammer.* MARVA *takes a breath and bashes the painting with the hammer. When she has finished they both stand back and contemplate their handiwork.*

We appear to have made rather a mess.

Pause.

I dread to think what Madge is going to say.

MARVA. I dread to think what Abi is going to say.

We went... we went... deep... deep into the archives.

FEN *and* MARVA *burst out laughing. They are laughing so hard that they have to hold their tummies.*

They both giggle uncontrollably for a while, then gain control of themselves.

We should tidy up.

FEN. We should. Let's do that.

They both rather half-heartedly shift the mess around, making absolutely no difference.

MARVA. What was a black electrician doing round here in the middle of nowhere?

FEN. Mmm?

MARVA. You said your dad named the blackamoor statue after him.

FEN. He just turned up one day, offered us favourable rates and then he was gone.

MARVA. In a puff of smoke.

FEN. That's right. (*Looking around at the messy room.*) It's not that bad. Madge will sort it out in the morning.

MARVA. Madge will put it all back together.

FEN. You're right. Let's call it a day. See you in the morning.

FEN and MARVA start to leave through separate exits. They both change their minds, turn and look at each other. They both have the same thought and quickly leave for the Dungeon together.

Scene Ten

The guest room. Later that night. ABI *is tossing and turning in bed. The house lets out a mournful moan, followed by a sigh, rattles and hammering.* ABI *sits bolt upright on the bed, unsettled. The house continues to groan.* ABI *gets out of bed and puts on her dressing gown. She sits on the edge of the bed, obviously afraid.*

ABI. What? What are you trying to say?

The groans and rattles quieten down.

A knock at the door.

Who is it?

Pause. Another knock on the door.

Who's there? What do you want?

The door slowly creaks opens.

The blackamoor statue is standing in the doorway.

ABI *screams.*

The blackamoor statue comes into the room.

We see that FEN *and* MARVA *are behind it.*

What are you doing? You scared me.

FEN. We need you to witness this. Marva says it can't be authenticated unless you witness it.

ABI. At two o'clock in the morning? I want to go to sleep. In my own bed. In a house that doesn't creak and groan with the aches and pains of old age. And where women don't creep about in the dead of night with hammers and blackamoor statues.

FEN (*to* MARVA). Do you want to do it?

FEN *hands* MARVA *the hammer.*

MARVA *raises the hammer but can't bear to bring it down onto Melvin. She tries again. Fails.*

MARVA. I can't. You do it.

FEN *takes the hammer and raises it.* ABI *gets between her and the statue.*

ABI. You can't go around destroying historical artefacts.

MARVA. My grandfather might be in there.

ABI. This is madness. How would he have got in there?

MARVA. His letters.

FEN. My brother moved Melvin into the Dungeon because he didn't want anyone to find what was hidden inside.

ABI. You know this for sure, do you?

FEN. It makes sense, doesn't it?

ABI (*to* MARVA). You resort to this nonsense, after everything you've been taught about evidence-backed proof?

MARVA. And what happens when all the evidence has been erased? What then?

ABI. It's never entirely erased, Marva. You'll always find it if you look. I made an incredible discovery tonight.

MARVA. What? What have you found?

ABI. In the diary. You won't believe this.

MARVA. What? Tell me.

ABI *speaks as she fetches the diary. She opens the diary to the relevant page.*

ABI. I was reading the journal again. I had my hand on the page, and I felt… Give me your hand.

ABI *takes* MARVA*'s hand and rubs it on the page.*

What do you feel?

MARVA. What am I supposed to feel?

ABI. So delicate. A mere trace. What happens when you press down hard with a pen on a piece of paper?

FEN. The ink pours out. It's a very simple technology.

ABI. What happens on the other side of the paper when you press down with a pen or pencil?

MARVA. It leaves an indentation.

MARVA *becomes aware of the indentation on the page.*

Oh my God.

FEN. What's going on?

ABI. When you press down hard with a pen on paper, which you might do if you were very emotional. You create pressure grooves, leaving an impression on the paper below.

MARVA. The impression remains even if you tear out the page and throw it away.

ABI. If you put tracing paper on the page and rub a pencil across it, like when you make a brass rubbing, it reveals what was written underneath.

FEN. Like a ghost of the page that was torn out?

ABI. Exactly that. A ghost page.

MARVA. What does Harford say on this ghost page?

ABI. He doesn't say anything. It's someone else who speaks.

MARVA. Who speaks, Abi?

ABI. It's hard to make everything out, but I retrieved some of the words. I've written them down. It's Black Sarah, Marva.

(*Reading.*) 'Harford liar… took one twin… your son and mine… gave Hannah. And I, Black Sarah, defy…'

FEN. What's going on?

ABI. Black Sarah is speaking to us from beyond the grave.

MARVA. You're sure that's what it says?

ABI. I'm sure. Here.

> ABI *gives* MARVA *the rubbing.* MARVA *holds the rubbing up to the light and reads.*

> In the diary entry Harford said that his firstborn son died, but then Hannah suddenly has a child. Black Sarah had twins. He took one of them away. You were right to question this, Marva.

MARVA. 'Took one twin. Your son and mine.'

ABI. She had access to the journal. She was a rebel. That's why she was always being punished. She scribbled this letter to him and he tore the page out so that no one else could see it, punished her for it.

MARVA (*to* ABI). Are you saying that Henry Harford was the son of an enslaved African?

ABI. When you go through Harford's inventories, he does indeed list the births of enslaved babies around the time of the birth of Hannah's child.

MARVA. Grandad was right. It all makes sense. He said that our family was directly descended from the Harfords. This proves it.

ABI. It's plausible.

Pause. We see the machines of MARVA*'s mind working.*

MARVA. The story of our heritage was passed down to my grandfather through generations of word of mouth. Nobody believed what he asserted because he had no tangible proof. But oral history is a valid source of evidence. This is… my God, Abi, this is…

FEN. Sorry, what? Are you saying that Black Sarah was the mother of Henry Harford's son?

ABI. That's the implication.

FEN. Then, doesn't that mean that I... Surely not... Really?... No – no... Really?

MARVA. This isn't about you, Fen.

FEN. I have always... I have always... I suppose I've always felt... I've always felt that we were different to other... That we were outsiders.

MARVA. This isn't your story.

ABI. Harford took poor Black Sarah's child and gave it to Hannah.

FEN. Are you saying that Black Sarah is my great-great-great-whatever-whatever-whatever-grandmother?

MARVA. This is my grandfather's story.

FEN. This morning I was plain old Fenella Harford. And now I'm... What am I? I am a descendant of Black Sarah. I need to... I'm just going to...

FEN *leaves.* MARVA *is open-mouthed.*

MARVA. What the actual fuck?

Scene Eleven

As FEN *gets ready, she listens to* Woman's Hour *on the radio. She ties a scarf of Ghanaian design around her neck.*

INTERVIEWER (*recorded*). It must have come as something of a shock when you discovered what you call the ghost letter. Can you tell us what emotions you experienced?

FEN (*recorded*). I don't think the words exist for my emotions. To be honest, I didn't believe it. I even had one of those ancestry DNA tests done.

INTERVIEWER (*recorded*). Fascinating. And do you mind telling us the outcome?

FEN. I don't mind telling you at all. The test revealed that traces of my Ghanaian ancestry remain in my blood. I am two per cent Ghanaian.

INTERVIEWER (*recorded*). And how does this impact on the work you're doing with Harford House?

FEN (*recorded*). It means that there's a hidden story to be told. And I intend to tell it.

The recording fades.

Scene Twelve

The Dungeon (now Fen's studio), Harford House. A few weeks after the discovery of the ghost page.

By the wall is a sculpture that has been covered with tarpaulin. FEN *and* MARVA *are alone in the Dungeon.* FEN *has the Ghanaian scarf around her shoulders (this is a subtle gesture, not over-the-top).*

MARVA *has just handed* FEN *a copy of a book.* FEN *considers the book.*

FEN. Congratulations. (*Reading the title.*) *Blood Lines.* That sounds a bit gory.

MARVA. It reflects my interest in the postcolonial gothic.

FEN. You've dedicated it to your grandfather. I bet he'd be ever so proud. I imagine Abi's over the moon.

MARVA. I could never have done anything like this without her encouragement.

FEN. You are a testament to her scheme. She's still coming, is she?

MARVA. I haven't seen her. Everyone goes their own way in the summer. There's an unspoken rule that we don't bother each other.

FEN. I hope she makes it.

Slight pause.

MARVA. I heard you on *Woman's Hour*.

FEN. I wasn't too provocative, was I? There may be more to the house than a pleasant afternoon tea, but I still want them to come for their scones.

MARVA. I can see it's a fine balancing act.

Slight pause.

You are two per cent Ghanaian.

FEN *breathes a sigh of relief.*

FEN. It's mad, isn't it?

MARVA. You are authenticated, Fen.

FEN (*unsure about what* MARVA *is saying*). Authenticated? I suppose so.

MARVA. I like your scarf.

FEN. It's not too much, is it? I don't want to be disrespectful, but I wanted to wear something that reflected the hidden history of Harford House.

FEN *waits for a response from* MARVA. *None is forthcoming.*

A flustered ABI *appears in the doorway.*

ABI. Sorry to be late. The taxi from the station took ages.

She enters the room.

You'd think the summer break would give us more time, but I'm even busier than I was during term time. We're off to Nigeria at the end of the week.

MARVA. It's good to see you, Abi.

ABI. You too. Are you excited about your book?

FEN. I was just admiring it.

ABI. It's not out already, is it?

MARVA. This isn't the actual book. I put the cover over an existing text to get a feel for what it's going to look like.

FEN. I'm so pleased that you are both able to come and celebrate Solfest with me.

ABI. I wouldn't want to miss it after everything you've told us about it.

FEN. This year promises to be our best yet. Have a programme.

FEN *hands* MARVA *and* ABI *programmes.* MARVA *reads.*

MARVA. Sidney Soul? How did you manage to get her?

FEN. Black Sarah seems to have captured the collective imagination.

ABI. The Elder Malidoma's healing ritual.

FEN. That's been cancelled. He was going to perform a ritual of reconciliation over Harford's statue, but he can't make it now.

MARVA. I'll bet Harford is relieved.

FEN. I'm going to make a speech instead. This is very different from festivals of years gone by. It's rattled quite a few cages, I can tell you.

MARVA. What do you mean?

FEN. The usual. There have been a few hate letters.

ABI. What a surprise.

Your text said you've finished your sculpture. Can we see it?

FEN. I am a little nervous to show you, but… of course.

FEN *lifts the tarpaulin to reveal the sculpture of a woman in a Ghanaian headdress who looks a little like* MARVA.

It's Black Sarah.

MARVA. It's beautiful, Fen.

ABI. You're very talented. She looks just like Marva.

FEN. Marva might have had some influence on it.

MARVA. Me? I don't look like that, do I?

ABI. Of course you do. You can't see yourself.

MARVA. I don't know what to say. I'm flattered.

FEN. I'm going to put her in the library. She'll replace the portrait of Harford. My plan is to convert the library into a museum and keep the diaries there. I've been talking to the

National Trust. I'm hoping that Harford House will pass into their ownership once I'm gone. The legacy will be preserved for the nation. Warts and all.

ABI. Your job is complete.

FEN. I can't tell you how anxious I have been, knowing that I am the last of the line and wondering what will happen to the estate once I am gone. But now I feel – you're right – a sense of completion.

Come on, let's raise a toast in memory of Black Sarah, shall we?

FEN fetches a bottle and paper cups, pours champagne.

For all she endured and survived. To Black Sarah.

FEN and MARVA raise their glasses. ABI doesn't join in.

ABI. I'm sorry. I can't do this. I've been trying to keep quiet because what I'm about to say is going to have terrible consequences. Not least for me, but for all of us, really.

MARVA. Abi?

ABI. I've fucked up. Really badly. I've made a very basic error and I don't know what to do about it. At the very least I'll be thought incompetent and at the worst I'll be done for academic misconduct.

MARVA. Surely not, Abi. You're so meticulous.

ABI. I thought that I might be able to pretend that it hadn't happened. But I can't. I just can't.

MARVA. Abi, tell us what's going on.

ABI. The pressure grooves on the ghost page are too deep, too distinct, to be authentic. It's so obvious…

FEN. What are you saying, Abi?

ABI. The ghost page could not have been made by Black Sarah or indeed Henry Harford. How did I miss it? Even a novice would have seen it straight away. That night was so strange. I was drunk. I never get drunk. I wanted it to be real. But days later when I sobered up, I realised that it couldn't be.

FEN. What are you talking about? Of course it's real. We all saw it with our own eyes. You saw it, didn't you, Marva?

ABI. We saw what we wanted to see. We all wanted it to be real, so it was.

FEN. I know what this is. You don't like it, do you, that I am now no longer just the descendant of an enslaver, but that, unlike you, I am as much a victim of the legacy of enslavement as Marva.

ABI (*half-laughing, half-shocked*). You? A victim of enslavement? I see you, Fen. I know what you've done. You're a fraud.

FEN. You cannot bear that my mixed heritage disrupts your neat trauma narrative.

You talk about sharing power but it's you who hold all the power. And now you're trying to…

ABI. You left that there for us to discover. It is a simple fraud because it leaves the ghost of an impression and you cannot authenticate a ghost impression.

FEN. I am not a fraud.

ABI. No? Look at you. Who appropriates a history of pain?

FEN. I have found a genuine purpose. I won't allow you to take it away from me. I am a descendant of Black Sarah. Now, if you will excuse me, I have to go and make a speech.

ABI. The ghost page is as inauthentic as your bloody Solfest.

But FEN *has gone.*

The heavy door slams shut.

Come back, Fen. You cannot claim a history that isn't yours.

MARVA *tries the dungeon door.*

MARVA. It's locked. She's fucking locked us in.

ABI. You're kidding. Let us out.

MARVA. She'll come back, won't she?

(*Calling.*) Help! Help!

ABI. Help! Help!

They are both banging on the door and frantically shouting for help as the scene ends.

Scene Thirteen

The Dungeon. Later.

We hear the sounds of the celebration, which sound more raucous. ABI *is seated on the ground while* MARVA *paces up and down.*

ABI. You're making me nervous.

MARVA. She can't keep us down here forever, can she?

ABI. Of course she can't.

MARVA. I bet she's gonna go all Karen on our arses and call the Feds, tell them that we're a couple of tiefs who invaded her dungeon.

ABI. I have no idea what you're talking about.

Pause.

MARVA. Our bodies are gonna rot down here. In a hundred years not a trace of us will remain. Except perhaps these trainers.

Pause. MARVA *starts pacing again.* MARVA *tries to muffle a laugh.*

ABI. What? What? Share the joke…

MARVA. This reminds me… it reminds me of how you used to lock me up in your spare bedroom to get me to write my thesis.

ABI *laughs.*

ABI. It was the only way to get you to stay in one place long enough to get any writing done.

Pause.

I got the shock of my life when I saw your legs dangling outside my window and then seeing you pelt off down the driveway.

Pause.

A hatch suddenly opens in the door of the Dungeon and two cardboard cartons of food are pushed through.

ABI *and* MARVA *rush to the door.*

MARVA. Hey, Madge! Let us out. Let us out, Madge!

But whoever left the food has gone. ABI *picks up one of the cartons. She peels off a label attached to it and reads.*

ABI. Jollof pasta.

MARVA. Is that a thing?

ABI. There's a logic to it.

ABI *starts to eat.*

Mmmmm. It's good. Try some.

MARVA. I'm not hungry.

As ABI *eats,* MARVA *continues to walk back and forth, tries the door.*

Pause.

Black people who fly too close to the sun always end up in prison.

Pause.

There was that black judge who ended up in prison, remember? And that black politician who diddled his expenses.

ABI. He diddled his expenses.

MARVA. He wasn't the only one. He was the only one who ended up in prison, though.

ABI. You're right. I used to dot every 'i' and cross every 't' and I've still ended up locked up. I can't believe I fell for it. When this gets out…

MARVA. Does it have to get out?

ABI. Of course it does.

MARVA. I won't tell anyone. I bet Fen won't either.

ABI. Are you suggesting that I ignore what I know, that we pretend the ghost page is real? That's academic misconduct.

MARVA. You're still hell-bent on sticking to their rules, aren't you? Wake up, Abi. Look at where you are. The ghost page is real.

ABI. We are not in the business of creating speculative history, Marva. Speculative history…

MARVA. It is not speculative history. Black Sarah's story is true.

ABI. All those years ago, when I first met you, when you were a child. I wanted to equip you with something that would lead you to freedom.

MARVA. I'm not the little feral girl you pulled off the street any more. I am not your experiment.

ABI. You were never feral.

MARVA. But you don't see me as your equal, do you?

ABI. Do you know how many times I had to talk the Dean down from getting rid of you? How do you think you got through that disciplinary?

MARVA. That was an absolute joke. How could I be accused of racism just because I raised a student's mark from a C to a B?

ABI. You didn't consult with the examiner.

MARVA. A black student was marked down and I corrected it.

ABI. The point is that I have had your back at times when you didn't even know it.

MARVA. I'll always be a child in your eyes, won't I? And don't think I don't know why. Deep down inside you think I'm inferior because my ancestors were sold into slavery and yours weren't. You're just like any other entitled person, you think that you earned the privilege you were born into.

ABI. I do not think of you as inferior.

MARVA. Even with the ghost letter you make the automatic assumption that Fen was responsible. Do you honestly think that Fen is capable of reconstructing such an artefact?

ABI (*realisation dawning*). Be careful what you say now, Marva.

MARVA. How exactly do you think she did it, mmm? How was she able to think herself into an enslaved woman's mind, to recreate fragments of her appeal to Harford? That she could even begin to imagine the rage behind her words let alone be able to transform that into the fragments of a believeable grammar…

ABI. I don't want to hear any more. You didn't… you couldn't. What have you done?

MARVA. I did it, and I'm proud of it.

ABI. I can't believe what I'm hearing.

MARVA. I rescued Black Sarah from Harford's erasure.

ABI *scrutinises* MARVA.

ABI. I've known you since you were a little girl. I can read your face. You're lying. Why are you covering up for Fen?

MARVA. I'm not lying.

ABI *gets up, holds* MARVA*'s face.* MARVA *can't meet her gaze.*

ABI. Look at me, Marva. Why can't you look at me?

MARVA *breaks away.*

Pause.

MARVA (*mumbles*). It was an accident.

ABI. What?

MARVA (*clearer*). It was an accident. I was so deeply in the work that I absentmindedly… I placed a sheet of scrap paper on the diary and I was thinking about Black Sarah and I just doodled… words… just came out of me…

ABI. Doodled? You mean, it wasn't even deliberate?

MARVA *shakes her head.* ABI *starts to laugh. She can't stop laughing, a mixture of genuine amusement and shock. She stops after a while.*

I spent years building a department, training young academics, sending them out into the world. Now it is all destroyed.

MARVA. Not if you confirm the authentication of Black Sarah's marginalia.

ABI. What the hell are you asking me to do?

MARVA. I'm asking you to tell the truth.

ABI. That's not even funny.

MARVA. You authenticated Harford's diaries.

ABI. Because they are authentic.

MARVA. Establishing the truth is more than just establishing that the cover of the diaries are of calfskin or that the pages bear the Turkey Mill watermark.

FEN (*offstage*). Recent discoveries have brought to our attention Harford's abject crimes during the slave trade era. Over the next five years, the Harford Foundation will fund works that aim to rectify the damage wrought by Harford's legacy.

MARVA. Oh, shut up, Fen. (*To* ABI.) Harford's journals lie by omission. There is only one moment of truth in that fucking diary…

FEN (*offstage*). I of all people would love to put this history behind me but my conscience tells me that I must not follow that instinct.

MARVA. I'll shut her up. Where is it?

ABI. What? What are you looking for?

MARVA *looks around the room.*

MARVA *finds the switch that controls the lights of Solfest.*

FEN (*offstage*). Our first initiative in this regard will be an annual grant to the Adeyemi Project run by Doctor Abi Adeyemi, which offers children of African origin academic support from primary school to postgraduation.

ABI*'s ears prick up.*

ABI. What's she saying about my project?

MARVA *'pulls the plug'. There is the sound of lights going pop on the estate.*

MARVA. The one moment of truth in the diaries is when he describes being enraged by Black Sarah's defiance and sends her to the outhouse. We know what happened in that dank dark room: he tortured and raped her. When you discovered the ghost page I felt as though Black Sarah had guided my hand, spoken through me. As though it wasn't an accident at all.

ABI. After everything I taught you about academic rigour, about checking and double-checking.

Pause.

MARVA. You can trace your ancestry back hundreds of years. I can't do that. My past was taken away from me and I need it. Abi, I need it. My parents are dead. My grandfather used to say that there was a direct line from the dirty needles in their arms to the plantations that our ancestors laboured on. I may have made a mistake but at least I brought Black Sarah to life.

We hear the distant sound of footsteps.

She's there in Harford's diaries. If you read between lines you'll see her. My history was stolen from me. I've nothing. Let me have this, Abi. Please let me have this.

ABI. All right, Marva. All right.

MARVA *retreats into a corner of the Dungeon. As* ABI *goes to comfort her, the door of the Dungeon suddenly opens and* FEN *appears in the doorway. She seems stunned.*

FEN. The lights went out. Phut. They're all running around in the dark. Total chaos.

FEN *pours herself a drink.*

I'm going to have to go on *Woman's Hour* again, aren't I? Come clean. Own up to creating the ghost page. I'll tell them, though... I'll tell them that my intentions were to reveal the untold secrets of Harford House.

MARVA. Are you saying you created the ghost page?

FEN. I tried to reveal what Harford tried to repress. It's... you know, it's speculative history.

ABI. Enough, Fen.

FEN. I'm saying that you were right when you accused me [*of faking the ghost page*].

MARVA. It was me, Fen. I created the ghost page.

FEN. Did you? (*To* ABI.) Did she?

ABI. All I know for sure is that Marva taught me that authentication is more than just about what can be seen or touched; that oral history is a valid source of evidence.

FEN. What's going on?

ABI. The ghost page is authenticated.

FEN. But you just said that Marva… didn't you just say…

ABI. The ghost page is authenticated, Fen.

FEN. I see.

Slight pause.

That's good, isn't it?

MARVA *stands up and moves towards the door.*

MARVA. Thank you, Abi.

ABI. Where are you going?

MARVA. Home.

FEN. You'll never find your way back in the dark.

MARVA. I know where I'm going.

ABI. We didn't finish our toast. We've got to make a toast.

ABI *hands* MARVA *a glass, takes one herself.*

FEN. What does this mean? Does it mean that I am still… that I am once again…

ABI. You are a descendant of Black Sarah. And Marva is a descendant of Henry Harford.

MARVA. Henry Harford? No. I am a descendant of Black Sarah.

ABI (*to* FEN). You keep saying that you are the last living heir of Henry Harford, but you're not, are you? Marva is.

FEN. Is she?

MARVA (*squirming with a sudden realisation*). When you're suddenly hit with the reality… I mean… ugh… Henry Harford?

FEN. She is, isn't she? Yes she is.

MARVA. I mean… I mean…

ABI. You were right, Fen. This Solfest has proved a very memorable celebration. Please, raise your glasses. To Black Sarah.

FEN. To Black Sarah.

They both look at MARVA.

MARVA (*with mixed emotions*). To Black Sarah.

They toast.

The house makes a noise.

MARVA *reacts as though she has just seen something.*

Did you both see that?

FEN. What?

MARVA. I just saw… Didn't you see it?

FEN *sees something.*

There is a stupefied look on FEN's *face.*

ABI *sees something. She opens her mouth in wonder.*

The house makes a sound, having the last word.

The stage goes black.

The play ends.